HIG

PROTEIN

FOOD LIST

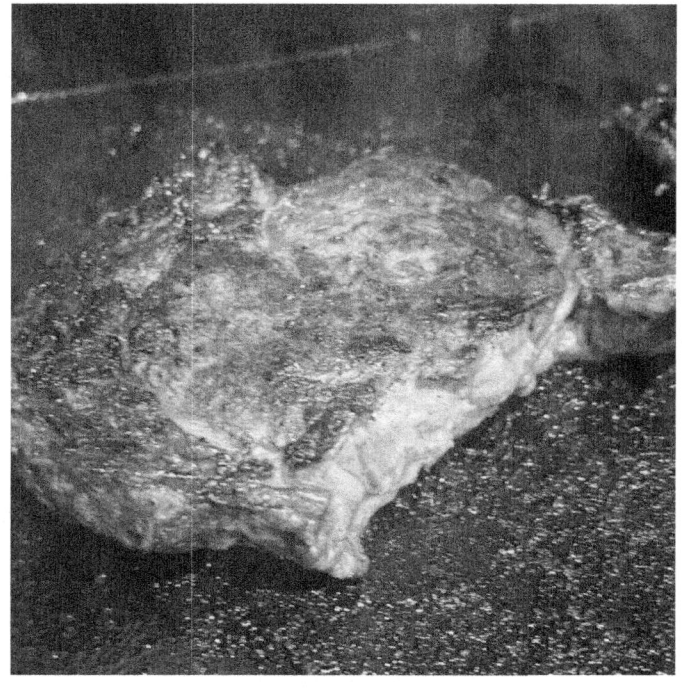

LORENE PEACHEY

Copyright © 2024 by Lorene Peachey

All rights reserved.

No part of this publication may be reproduced, stored in a retrieval system, or transmitted, in any form or by any means, electronic, mechanical, photocopying, recording or otherwise, without the prior written permission of the copyright holder.

This book is sold subject to the condition that it shall not, by way of trade or otherwise, be lent, re-sold, hired out or otherwise circulated without the publisher's prior consent in any form of binding or cover other than that in which it is published and without a similar condition including this condition being imposed on the subsequent purchaser.

DISCLAIMER

The content within this book reflects my thoughts, experiences, and beliefs. It is meant for informational and entertainment purposes. While I have taken great care to provide accurate information, I cannot guarantee the absolute correctness or applicability of the content to every individual or situation. Please consult with relevant professionals for advice specific to your needs.

TO GAIN ACCESS TO MORE BOOK BY THE AUTHOR SCAN THE QR CODE

TABLE OF CONTENTS

INTRODUCTION

In the enchanting world of nutrition, where flavors dance on the taste buds and health intertwines with every bite, I am your guide— Lorene Peachey, a devoted nutritionist with a passion for crafting a symphony of delicious, high-protein recipes. My journey into the realm of culinary wellness began not as a mere profession but as a lifelong commitment to unravel the secrets of nourishing the body and soul.

As I take you through the pages of this book, envision my years of dedication, my kitchen transformed into a laboratory of taste, my utensils wielded like magic wands, conjuring recipes that not only satisfy the palate but also nurture the body. For the past 25 years, I have delved deep into the world of nutritional alchemy, seeking the perfect combination of ingredients that not only satiate hunger but elevate well-being to new heights.

"Why devote a lifetime to understanding food?" you might wonder. The answer lies in the profound connection between what we consume and how we feel. Food is not just sustenance; it is an art, a science, a healer. Each ingredient has a story, and every recipe whispers secrets of vitality and longevity. It was this realization that led me on a quest to explore the potential of high-protein foods, unlocking their treasures for a healthier, more vibrant life.

Imagine awakening each morning to the aroma of a protein-packed breakfast, a plate filled with scrambled eggs kissed by the morning sun, and a symphony of berries that burst with flavor. The question is not merely what you eat but how it transforms you. How does a meal resonate with your spirit, replenish your energy, and sculpt the masterpiece that is your body?

Let's ponder the consequences of an unhealthy diet, a symphony played in discord. What happens when we surrender to the allure of processed foods, sugary temptations, and empty calories? Picture a garden untended, flowers wilting, and weeds thriving. The body responds in much the same way. It craves nutrients, it begs for sustenance, and it protests with fatigue, lethargy, and a myriad of health issues. Is this the life you envisioned?

Now, let me whisk you away from the shadowy corners of unhealthy choices into the luminous world of high-protein delights. Here, the benefits are abundant, the flavors robust, and the consequences are a distant echo. High-protein foods, like culinary superheroes, come to your rescue, offering more than just a tantalizing taste. They pave the way for a stronger immune system, leaner muscles, and a metabolism that hums with efficiency.

But why focus on high-protein foods, you ask? Imagine proteins as the architects of your body—a crucial component in building and repairing tissues, creating enzymes and hormones, and providing the energy needed for day-to-day activities. Proteins are the backbone of a healthy diet, the silent heroes that work tirelessly behind the scenes to keep you moving, thinking, and thriving.

As we venture into the heart of this book, let me be your culinary companion, weaving tales of delectable recipes that embody both flavor and nutrition. Let's explore the world of lean meats, succulent seafood, hearty legumes, and the magic of nuts and seeds. Each page unfolds a new chapter, a feast for the eyes and a celebration for the senses.

In this friendly and inviting space, you'll discover recipes that not only nourish your body but also satisfy your culinary cravings. Picture a savory quinoa bowl adorned with vibrant vegetables, a delightful dance of flavors and textures that beckon you to embrace a healthier lifestyle. Can you feel the anticipation building within you?

But it's not just about the physical transformation; it's about the emotional journey. How will these recipes make you feel? Will they evoke memories of shared meals with loved ones, spark moments of joy in your kitchen, and become the catalyst for a deeper connection with your body? Food is more than sustenance; it's an emotional journey, a reflection of our culture, and a bridge to our memories.

And here's the beauty of it—high-protein foods offer a splendid array of options, accommodating diverse tastes, preferences, and dietary needs. Whether you're a lover of vibrant salads, a devotee of hearty stews, or a connoisseur of international flavors, this book is your passport to a culinary adventure that aligns with your unique palate and lifestyle.

As we embark on this gastronomic voyage, let's not forget the simplicity of it all. High-protein foods don't demand complicated rituals or obscure ingredients. They invite you to embrace the simplicity of nourishment, the joy of preparing a meal that not only supports your health goals but also becomes a cherished moment in your day.

So, dear reader, are you ready to embark on this flavorful journey with me? Can you feel the excitement building, the anticipation of discovering recipes that will not only tantalize your taste buds but also transform the way you approach food? Open your heart to the possibilities, and let high-protein foods be your companions on the path to a healthier, happier you.

Together, let's savor the flavors of wellness, revel in the joy of nourishment, and create a tapestry of high-protein recipes that will define your culinary legacy. Welcome to a world where food is not just sustenance but a celebration of life.

CHAPTER 1

PURPOSE OF A HIGH-PROTEIN DIET

A high-protein diet has gained widespread popularity for its numerous health benefits and its role in supporting various bodily functions. Proteins are essential macronutrients composed of amino acids, which play a crucial role in the structure and function of the body. This article explores the purpose of a high-protein diet and the benefits associated with consuming foods rich in protein.

Purpose of a High-Protein Diet:

1. **Muscle Building and Repair:**

    - Protein is a fundamental building block for muscles, and consuming an adequate amount is crucial for muscle development and repair.

    - Athletes and individuals engaged in regular physical activity often rely on a high-protein diet to support muscle growth and recovery after exercise.

2. **Weight Management:**

   - High-protein foods contribute to satiety, helping individuals feel fuller for longer periods.

   - This can aid in weight management by reducing overall calorie intake and promoting fat loss, as the body expends more energy digesting protein compared to fats and carbohydrates.

3. **Metabolism Support:**

   - Protein has a higher thermic effect compared to other macronutrients, meaning the body burns more calories during digestion and absorption of protein.

   - A high-protein diet may support a faster metabolism, potentially assisting in weight loss and maintenance.

4. **Blood Sugar Regulation:**

   - Including protein in meals can help stabilize blood sugar levels by slowing down the absorption of carbohydrates.

   - This can be particularly beneficial for individuals with diabetes or those looking to manage their blood sugar levels.

Benefits of Consuming High-Protein Foods:

1. **Improved Muscle Health:**

    -   Adequate protein intake supports the maintenance and development of lean muscle mass.

    -   This is crucial for overall strength, physical performance, and the prevention of age-related muscle loss.

2. **Enhanced Satiety and Appetite Control:**

    -   Protein-rich foods have been shown to increase feelings of fullness and reduce overall food intake.

    -   This can be advantageous for those aiming to control their appetite and make healthier food choices.

3. **Support for Bone Health:**

    -   Some proteins, such as collagen, are essential for maintaining bone strength and integrity.

    -   Including a variety of protein sources in the diet contributes to overall bone health.

4. **Optimal Immune Function:**

- Proteins play a key role in the immune system, as antibodies and immune cells are composed of amino acids.

- A high-protein diet supports the body's ability to defend against infections and illnesses.

Contact the Author

Thank you for reading my book! I would love to hear from you, whether you have feedback, questions, or just want to share your thoughts. Your feedback means a lot to me and helps me improve as a writer.

Please don't hesitate to reach out to me through

lorenepeachey@gmail.com

I look forward to connecting with my readers and appreciate your support in this literary journey. Your thoughts and comments are valuable to me.

CHAPTER 2

UNDERSTANDING PROTEIN

Protein is a fundamental macronutrient that plays a crucial role in maintaining and supporting various physiological functions within the human body. This article delves into the importance of protein and provides insights into the recommended daily intake for optimal health.

Importance of Protein in the Body:

1. **Structural Component:**

    - Proteins are essential building blocks for tissues, muscles, organs, and even DNA.

    - They contribute to the structural integrity of cells, providing the framework for growth, repair, and maintenance.

2. **Enzymatic Functions:**

    - Many enzymes, which are essential for facilitating biochemical reactions, are proteins.

    - Enzymes enable metabolic processes, including digestion, energy production, and cellular repair.

3. **Immune System Support:**

- Antibodies, vital components of the immune system that defend the body against infections and diseases, are composed of proteins.

- A sufficient protein intake is crucial for the proper functioning of the immune system.

4. **Transportation and Storage:**

- Proteins play a role in transporting molecules, such as oxygen in the blood (hemoglobin) and nutrients within cells.

- They also act as storage molecules for essential substances, ensuring a steady supply when needed.

5. **Hormonal Regulation:**

- Certain proteins function as hormones, acting as messengers that regulate various physiological processes.

- Hormones influence growth, metabolism, and other vital functions in the body.

Recommended Daily Protein Intake:

1. **General Guidelines:**

   - The recommended daily protein intake varies based on factors such as age, sex, weight, activity level, and overall health.

   - On average, adult individuals are advised to consume about 0.8 grams of protein per kilogram of body weight per day.

2. **Physical Activity and Goals:**

   - Athletes, individuals engaged in regular intense exercise, or those looking to build muscle may require higher protein intake.

   - Recommendations for athletes can range from 1.2 to 2.2 grams of protein per kilogram of body weight.

3. **Special Populations:**

   - Pregnant and lactating women, as well as older adults, may have specific protein requirements to support their unique physiological needs.

   - Consultation with healthcare professionals or nutritionists is recommended for personalized guidance.

4. **Protein Quality:**

- It's not only the quantity but also the quality of protein that matters. Sources such as meat, fish, eggs, dairy, legumes, and plant-based protein options contribute to a well-balanced protein intake.

CHAPTER 3

ANIMAL-BASED PROTEIN

SOURCES

Lean Meats

1. **Chicken Breast:**

   - *Nutritional Information (per 3.5 oz):*

     - Calories: 165

     - Protein: 31g

     - Fat: 3.6g

     - Iron: 1.1mg

2. **Turkey Breast:**

   - *Nutritional Information (per 3.5 oz):*

     - Calories: 135

     - Protein: 30g

     - Fat: 1g

     - Iron: 1.4mg

3. **Lean Ground Beef (90% lean):**

- *Nutritional Information (per 3.5 oz):*

    - Calories: 184

    - Protein: 20g

    - Fat: 11g

    - Iron: 2.3mg

4. **Pork Tenderloin:**

- *Nutritional Information (per 3.5 oz):*

    - Calories: 143

    - Protein: 24g

    - Fat: 4.5g

    - Iron: 1mg

5. **Chicken Thigh (skinless):**

- *Nutritional Information (per 3.5 oz):*

    - Calories: 209

    - Protein: 26g

    - Fat: 12g

    - Iron: 1.1mg

6. **Lean Ground Chicken:**

- *Nutritional Information (per 3.5 oz):*

  - Calories: 165

  - Protein: 24g

  - Fat: 8g

  - Iron: 1.2mg

7. **Venison (deer meat):**

- *Nutritional Information (per 3.5 oz):*

  - Calories: 158

  - Protein: 30g

  - Fat: 3g

  - Iron: 6.2mg

8. **Lean Ground Turkey (93% lean):**

- *Nutritional Information (per 3.5 oz):*

  - Calories: 176

  - Protein: 21g

  - Fat: 10g

  - Iron: 1.6mg

Fish and Seafood

1. **Salmon:**

   - *Nutritional Information (per 3.5 oz):*

     - Calories: 206

     - Protein: 22g

     - Fat: 13g

     - Omega-3 Fatty Acids: 2.3g

2. **Tuna (Yellowfin, cooked):**

   - *Nutritional Information (per 3.5 oz):*

     - Calories: 109

     - Protein: 25g

     - Fat: 1.3g

     - Vitamin D: 2.4mcg

3. **Cod:**

- *Nutritional Information (per 3.5 oz):*

    - Calories: 82

    - Protein: 18g

    - Fat: 1g

    - Vitamin B12: 1.1mcg

4. **Shrimp:**

- *Nutritional Information (per 3.5 oz):*

    - Calories: 99

    - Protein: 24g

    - Fat: 1.7g

    - Selenium: 34mcg

5. **Sardines (canned in oil):**

- *Nutritional Information (per 3.5 oz):*

    - Calories: 208

    - Protein: 25g

    - Fat: 11g

    - Calcium: 490mg

6. **Mackerel:**

- *Nutritional Information (per 3.5 oz):*

    - Calories: 305

    - Protein: 18g

    - Fat: 25g

    - Omega-3 Fatty Acids: 4.5g

7. **Halibut:**

- *Nutritional Information (per 3.5 oz):*

    - Calories: 140

    - Protein: 23g

    - Fat: 5g

    - Vitamin D: 2.7mcg

8. **Lobster:**

- *Nutritional Information (per 3.5 oz):*

    - Calories: 89

    - Protein: 17g

    - Fat: 1.1g

    - Selenium: 31mcg

9. **Trout:**

- *Nutritional Information (per 3.5 oz):*

    - Calories: 168

    - Protein: 22g

    - Fat: 9g

    - Omega-3 Fatty Acids: 1.8g

10. **Clams:**

- *Nutritional Information (per 3.5 oz):*

    - Calories: 74

    - Protein: 13g

    - Fat: 1.5g

    - Iron: 3mg

Dairy Products

1. **Greek Yogurt:**

   - *Nutritional Information (per 6 oz):*

     - Calories: 100

     - Protein: 15g

     - Fat: 0g

     - Calcium: 150mg

2. **Cottage Cheese:**

   - *Nutritional Information (per 1 cup):*

     - Calories: 220

     - Protein: 28g

     - Fat: 10g

     - Calcium: 220mg

3. **Mozzarella Cheese:**

- *Nutritional Information (per 1 oz):*

  - Calories: 80

  - Protein: 6g

  - Fat: 6g

  - Calcium: 143mg

4. **Cheddar Cheese:**

- *Nutritional Information (per 1 oz):*

  - Calories: 115

  - Protein: 7g

  - Fat: 9g

  - Calcium: 204mg

5. **Skim Milk:**

- *Nutritional Information (per 1 cup):*

  - Calories: 83

  - Protein: 8g

  - Fat: 0g

  - Calcium: 299mg

6. **Swiss Cheese:**

   - *Nutritional Information (per 1 oz):*

     - Calories: 111

     - Protein: 8g

     - Fat: 9g

     - Calcium: 224mg

7. **Low-Fat Yogurt (plain):**

   - *Nutritional Information (per 6 oz):*

     - Calories: 100

     - Protein: 10g

     - Fat: 2g

     - Calcium: 250mg

8. **Ricotta Cheese:**

   - *Nutritional Information (per 1 oz):*

     - Calories: 49

     - Protein: 3g

     - Fat: 4g

     - Calcium: 68mg

9. **Whole Milk:**

- *Nutritional Information (per 1 cup):*

    - Calories: 150

    - Protein: 8g

    - Fat: 8g

    - Calcium: 276mg

10. **Protein Fortified Almond Milk:**

- *Nutritional Information (per 1 cup):*

    - Calories: 80

    - Protein: 5g

    - Fat: 2.5g

    - Calcium: 450mg

CHAPTER 4

PLANT-BASED PROTEIN

SOURCES

Legumes and Pulses

1. **Lentils:**

    - *Nutritional Information (per 1 cup, cooked):*

        - Calories: 230

        - Protein: 18g

        - Fiber: 16g

        - Iron: 6.6mg

2. **Chickpeas (Garbanzo Beans):**

    - *Nutritional Information (per 1 cup, cooked):*

        - Calories: 269

        - Protein: 15g

        - Fiber: 13g

        - Iron: 4.7mg

3. **Black Beans:**

- *Nutritional Information (per 1 cup, cooked):*

    - Calories: 227

    - Protein: 15g

    - Fiber: 15g

    - Iron: 3.6mg

4. **Kidney Beans:**

- *Nutritional Information (per 1 cup, cooked):*

    - Calories: 225

    - Protein: 15g

    - Fiber: 11g

    - Iron: 4mg

5. **Split Peas:**

- *Nutritional Information (per 1 cup, cooked):*

    - Calories: 231

    - Protein: 16g

    - Fiber: 16g

    - Iron: 2.5mg

6. **Edamame (Soybeans):**

- *Nutritional Information (per 1 cup, cooked):*

  - Calories: 188

  - Protein: 18g

  - Fiber: 8g

  - Iron: 2.1mg

7. **Pinto Beans:**

- *Nutritional Information (per 1 cup, cooked):*

  - Calories: 245

  - Protein: 15g

  - Fiber: 15g

  - Iron: 3.6mg

8. **Green Peas:**

- *Nutritional Information (per 1 cup, cooked):*

  - Calories: 62

  - Protein: 4g

  - Fiber: 9g

  - Iron: 1.5mg

9. **Black-eyed Peas:**

- *Nutritional Information (per 1 cup, cooked):*

    - Calories: 160

    - Protein: 5g

    - Fiber: 5g

    - Iron: 2.2mg

10. **Cannellini Beans:**

- *Nutritional Information (per 1 cup, cooked):*

    - Calories: 218

    - Protein: 15g

    - Fiber: 13g

    - Iron: 3.6mg

Nuts and Seeds

1. **Almonds:**

    - *Nutritional Information (per 1 oz, about 23 almonds):*

        - Calories: 160

        - Protein: 6g

        - Fiber: 3.5g

        - Vitamin E: 7.3mg

2. **Peanuts:**

    - *Nutritional Information (per 1 oz, about 28 peanuts):*

        - Calories: 161

        - Protein: 7g

        - Fiber: 2.5g

        - Folate: 40mcg

3. **Sunflower Seeds:**

- *Nutritional Information (per 1 oz):*

    - Calories: 160

    - Protein: 5.5g

    - Fiber: 3g

    - Vitamin B6: 0.3mg

4. **Chia Seeds:**

- *Nutritional Information (per 1 oz):*

    - Calories: 138

    - Protein: 4.7g

    - Fiber: 9.8g

    - Omega-3 Fatty Acids: 4.9g

5. **Pumpkin Seeds (Pepitas):**

- *Nutritional Information (per 1 oz):*

    - Calories: 151

    - Protein: 7g

    - Fiber: 1.7g

    - Magnesium: 150mg

6. **Walnuts:**

- *Nutritional Information (per 1 oz, about 14 halves):*

    - Calories: 185

    - Protein: 4g

    - Fiber: 2g

    - Omega-3 Fatty Acids: 2.6g

7. **Cashews:**

- *Nutritional Information (per 1 oz, about 18 cashews):*

    - Calories: 157

    - Protein: 5g

    - Fiber: 1g

    - Iron: 1.7mg

8. **Flaxseeds:**

- *Nutritional Information (per 1 oz):*

    - Calories: 150

    - Protein: 5g

    - Fiber: 8g

    - Omega-3 Fatty Acids: 6.4g

9. **Hazelnuts:**

- *Nutritional Information (per 1 oz, about 21 hazelnuts):*

    - Calories: 176

    - Protein: 4g

    - Fiber: 3g

    - Vitamin E: 4.3mg

10. **Sesame Seeds:**

- *Nutritional Information (per 1 oz):*

    - Calories: 160

    - Protein: 5g

    - Fiber: 4g

    - Calcium: 277mg

CHAPTER 5

PROTEIN-PACKED GRAINS

1. **Quinoa:**

   - *Nutritional Information (per 1 cup, cooked):*

     - Calories: 222

     - Protein: 8g

     - Fiber: 5g

     - Iron: 2.8mg

2. **Farro:**

   - *Nutritional Information (per 1 cup, cooked):*

     - Calories: 220

     - Protein: 7g

     - Fiber: 3g

     - Iron: 2.4mg

3. **Buckwheat Groats:**

- *Nutritional Information (per 1 cup, cooked):*

    - Calories: 155

    - Protein: 6g

    - Fiber: 5g

    - Iron: 1.3mg

4. **Amaranth:**

- *Nutritional Information (per 1 cup, cooked):*

    - Calories: 251

    - Protein: 9g

    - Fiber: 5g

    - Iron: 5.2mg

5. **Barley:**

- *Nutritional Information (per 1 cup, cooked):*

    - Calories: 193

    - Protein: 3.5g

    - Fiber: 6g

    - Iron: 1.3mg

6. **Brown Rice:**

- *Nutritional Information (per 1 cup, cooked):*

    - Calories: 215

    - Protein: 5g

    - Fiber: 3.5g

    - Iron: 1.2mg

7. **Millet:**

- *Nutritional Information (per 1 cup, cooked):*

    - Calories: 207

    - Protein: 6g

    - Fiber: 2.3g

    - Iron: 1.1mg

8. **Spelt:**

- *Nutritional Information (per 1 cup, cooked):*

    - Calories: 246

    - Protein: 10g

    - Fiber: 7.5g

    - Iron: 3.2mg

9. **Freekeh:**

- *Nutritional Information (per 1 cup, cooked):*

    - Calories: 220

    - Protein: 8g

    - Fiber: 4g

    - Iron: 3.7mg

10. **Teff:**

- *Nutritional Information (per 1 cup, cooked):*

    - Calories: 255

    - Protein: 10g

    - Fiber: 7g

    - Iron: 5.8mg

CHAPTER 6

LOW PROTEIN FOODS

1. **Iceberg Lettuce:**

   - *Nutritional Information (per 1 cup, shredded):*

     - Calories: 10

     - Protein: 0.5g

     - Fiber: 0.7g

2. **Cucumber:**

   - *Nutritional Information (per 1 cup, sliced):*

     - Calories: 16

     - Protein: 0.8g

     - Fiber: 0.7g

3. **Tomatoes:**

- *Nutritional Information (per 1 medium-sized tomato):*

  - Calories: 22

  - Protein: 1g

  - Fiber: 1.5g

4. **Bell Peppers:**

- *Nutritional Information (per 1 cup, sliced):*

  - Calories: 19

  - Protein: 0.7g

  - Fiber: 2.5g

5. **Zucchini:**

- *Nutritional Information (per 1 cup, sliced):*

  - Calories: 20

  - Protein: 1.4g

  - Fiber: 0.6g

6. **Strawberries:**

- *Nutritional Information (per 1 cup, whole):*

    - Calories: 49

    - Protein: 1g

    - Fiber: 3g

7. **White Bread:**

- *Nutritional Information (per 1 slice):*

    - Calories: 69

    - Protein: 2g

    - Fiber: 0.8g

8. **White Rice (cooked):**

- *Nutritional Information (per 1 cup):*

    - Calories: 205

    - Protein: 4.3g

    - Fiber: 0.6g

9. **Bananas:**

- *Nutritional Information (per medium-sized banana):*

    - Calories: 105

    - Protein: 1.3g

    - Fiber: 3.1g

10. **Apples:**

- *Nutritional Information (per medium-sized apple):*

    - Calories: 95

    - Protein: 0.5g

    - Fiber: 4.4g

CONCLUSION

As we reach the final pages of this culinary journey, my heart swells with gratitude for the time we've spent together exploring the realm of high-protein delights. I hope these recipes have not only invigorated your taste buds but also ignited a passion for nourishing your body in a way that sparks joy and vitality.

In the tapestry of life, each meal is a brushstroke, and with every bite, you contribute to the masterpiece that is your well-being. The high-protein recipes shared in this book are not merely a collection of ingredients and instructions; they are an invitation to embrace a lifestyle that harmonizes pleasure and health, flavor and nutrition.

As you savor the flavors of these recipes, I encourage you to listen to your body's whispers. How does it respond to the wholesome goodness you've indulged in? Do you feel a surge of energy, a revitalization that courses through your veins? This is the magic of nourishing your body with intention and care.

Feedback, dear reader, is the heartbeat of any author's journey. Your thoughts, experiences, and insights are invaluable. I invite you to share your culinary adventures with these high-protein recipes. Did you discover a favorite dish that has become a staple in your kitchen? How did these recipes transform your relationship with food?

Your feedback not only fuels my passion for creating recipes that resonate with you but also fosters a sense of community—a shared space where we can celebrate the joys and challenges of embracing a healthier lifestyle. Together, we are not just readers and authors; we are companions on a shared quest for wellness.

In the spirit of openness and growth, I welcome your thoughts on how this book can continue to serve you better. Are there specific topics you'd like to explore further? Are there dietary preferences or restrictions that could be better accommodated? Your input is not only valued but cherished.

As you step away from these pages and into your kitchen, remember that every meal is an opportunity to express love for yourself and those around you. Let the act of preparing and savoring these high-protein recipes be a form of self-care, a reminder that you deserve to nourish your body with the best nature has to offer.

May your culinary adventures be filled with joy, may your plates be vibrant canvases of health, and may you continue to savor the rich tapestry of flavors that life has to offer. Thank you for entrusting me with a moment of your journey. Until we meet again, happy cooking, happy nourishing, and happy living.

BONUS CHAPTER 1

HIGH PROTEIN RECIPES

Grilled Chicken Breast with Lemon and Herbs

Cooking Time: 20 minutes

Servings: 4

Ingredients:

- 4 boneless, skinless chicken breasts

- 2 tablespoons olive oil

- 2 tablespoons fresh lemon juice

- 1 teaspoon dried oregano

Instructions:

1. Preheat the grill to medium-high heat.

2. In a bowl, mix olive oil, lemon juice, oregano, salt, and pepper.

3. Brush the chicken breasts with the mixture.

4. Grill for 8-10 minutes per side or until fully cooked.

5. Serve with your favorite veggies.

Nutritional Information: 250 calories, 40g protein, 10g fat, 2g carbohydrates

Quinoa and Black Bean Bowl

Cooking Time: 25 minutes

Servings: 3

Ingredients:

- 1 cup quinoa

- 1 can black beans, drained and rinsed

- 1 cup cherry tomatoes, halved

- 1 cup cucumber, diced

- 1/4 cup red onion, finely chopped

- 1/4 cup feta cheese, crumbled

Instructions:

1. Cook quinoa according to package instructions.

2. In a large bowl, combine quinoa, black beans, cherry tomatoes, cucumber, red onion, and feta.

3. Toss with your favorite vinaigrette.

Nutritional Information: 320 calories, 15g protein, 8g fat, 50g carbohydrates

Baked Salmon with Dill and Garlic

Cooking Time: 15 minutes

Servings: 2

Ingredients:

- 2 salmon fillets

- 2 tablespoons olive oil

- 2 cloves garlic, minced

- 1 tablespoon fresh dill, chopped

- Salt and pepper to taste

Instructions:

1. Preheat the oven to 400°F (200°C).

2. Place salmon fillets on a baking sheet.

3. Mix olive oil, garlic, dill, salt, and pepper in a bowl.

4. Brush the mixture over the salmon.

5. Bake for 12-15 minutes or until the salmon flakes easily.

Nutritional Information: 300 calories, 30g protein, 18g fat, 2g carbohydrates

Chickpea and Spinach Curry

Cooking Time: 30 minutes

Servings: 4

Ingredients:

- 2 cans chickpeas, drained
- 2 cups fresh spinach
- 1 onion, finely chopped
- 2 tomatoes, diced
- 3 cloves garlic, minced
- 1 tablespoon curry powder
- 1 cup coconut milk

Instructions:

1. In a large pan, sauté onion and garlic until golden.

2. Add chickpeas, tomatoes, and curry powder. Cook for 5 minutes.

3. Pour in coconut milk and simmer for 15 minutes.

4. Stir in spinach and cook until wilted.

Nutritional Information: 380 calories, 18g protein, 14g fat, 50g carbohydrates

Turkey and Quinoa Stuffed Peppers

Cooking Time: 45 minutes

Servings: 6

Ingredients:

- 1 cup quinoa
- 1.5 pounds ground turkey
- 6 bell peppers, halved and seeds removed
- 1 can black beans, drained
- 1 cup corn kernels
- 1 cup salsa
- 1 teaspoon cumin

Instructions:

1. Cook quinoa according to package instructions.

2. In a skillet, brown ground turkey. Add cumin, salt, and pepper.

3. Mix cooked quinoa, black beans, corn, salsa, and turkey.

4. Stuff bell peppers with the mixture.

5. Bake at 375°F (190°C) for 25-30 minutes.

Nutritional Information: 320 calories, 25g protein, 8g fat, 40g carbohydrates

Lentil and Vegetable Stir-Fry

Cooking Time: 25 minutes

Servings: 4

Ingredients:

- 1 cup dry lentils
- 2 cups broccoli florets
- 1 red bell pepper, sliced
- 1 carrot, julienned
- 2 tablespoons soy sauce
- 1 tablespoon sesame oil
- 1 tablespoon ginger, minced

Instructions:

1. Cook lentils according to package instructions.

2. In a wok, stir-fry broccoli, bell pepper, and carrot in sesame oil.

3. Add cooked lentils, soy sauce, and ginger. Stir until heated through.

4. Serve over brown rice.

Nutritional Information: 280 calories, 18g protein, 8g fat, 35g carbohydrates

Tofu and Vegetable Skewers

Cooking Time: 30 minutes

Servings: 4

Ingredients:

- 1 block firm tofu, cubed

- 2 bell peppers, cut into chunks

- 1 zucchini, sliced

- 1 red onion, sliced

- 2 tablespoons olive oil

- 2 tablespoons balsamic vinegar

- 1 teaspoon dried thyme

- Salt and pepper to taste

Instructions:

1. Preheat the grill or oven to medium-high heat.

2. Thread tofu, bell peppers, zucchini, and red onion onto skewers.

3. Mix olive oil, balsamic vinegar, thyme, salt, and pepper in a bowl.

4. Brush the skewers with the mixture.

5. Grill or bake for 15-20 minutes, turning occasionally.

Nutritional Information: 250 calories, 15g protein, 12g fat, 20g carbohydrates

Egg White and Vegetable Omelette

Cooking Time: 15 minutes

Servings: 2

Ingredients:

- 4 egg whites

- 1 cup spinach

- 1 tomato, diced

- 1/4 cup feta cheese, crumbled

- 1/2 teaspoon olive oil

- Salt and pepper to taste

Instructions:

1. Whisk egg whites in a bowl until frothy.

2. In a non-stick pan, sauté spinach and tomatoes in olive oil.

3. Pour egg whites over the vegetables.

4. Cook until set, then fold the omelette.

5. Sprinkle feta cheese on top.

Nutritional Information: 180 calories, 20g protein, 8g fat, 8g carbohydrates

High-Protein Pasta Salad

Cooking Time: 15 minutes

Servings: 4

Ingredients:

- 8 oz high-protein pasta

- 1 cup cherry tomatoes, halved

- 1 cucumber, diced

- 1/2 cup Kalamata olives, sliced

- 1/4 cup red onion, finely chopped

- 1/4 cup feta cheese, crumbled

- 2 tablespoons olive oil

- 1 tablespoon balsamic vinegar

- Salt and pepper to taste

Instructions:

1. Cook pasta according to package instructions.

2. In a large bowl, combine pasta, cherry tomatoes, cucumber, olives, red onion, and feta.

3. In a small bowl, whisk together olive oil, balsamic vinegar, salt, and pepper.

4. Toss the pasta salad with the dressing.

Nutritional Information: 350 calories, 20g protein, 12g fat, 40g carbohydrates

Chicken and Quinoa Burrito Bowl

Cooking Time: 30 minutes

Servings: 4

Ingredients:

- 1 cup quinoa

- 1 pound chicken breast, grilled and sliced

- 1 can black beans, drained and rinsed

- 1 cup corn kernels

- 1 avocado, sliced

- 1/2 cup salsa

- 1/4 cup Greek yogurt

- Fresh cilantro for garnish

Instructions:

1. Cook quinoa according to package instructions.

2. Assemble bowls with quinoa, grilled chicken, black beans, corn, avocado, salsa, and a dollop of Greek yogurt.

3. Garnish with fresh cilantro.

Nutritional Information: 420 calories, 30g protein, 15g fat, 45g carbohydrates

IF YOU WANT MORE RECIPES, YOU CAN CHECK OUT
OTHER BOOKS BY THE AUTHOR

MEDITERRANEAN INSTANT POT COOKBOOK FOR
WOMEN

GLUTEN-FREE COOKBOOK FOR WOMEN

GLUTEN-FREE COOKBOOK FOR KIDS

GLUTEN-FREE AIR FRYER COOKBOOK

TO GET ACCESS TO MORE BOOKS BY THE AUTHOR
SCAN THE QR CODE

BONUS CHAPTER 2

21 DAY MEAL PLAN

Day	Breakfast	Lunch	Dinner
1	Scrambled Eggs with Spinach	Quinoa and Black Bean Bowl	Grilled Chicken Breast with Salad
2	Greek Yogurt Parfait	Lentil and Vegetable Stir-Fry	Baked Salmon with Lemon and Herbs
3	Protein Smoothie with Berries	Tofu and Vegetable Skewers	Chickpea and Spinach Curry
4	Oatmeal with Almond Butter	Turkey and Quinoa Stuffed Peppers	Egg White and Vegetable Omelette
5	Cottage Cheese with Pineapple	High-Protein Pasta Salad	Farro and Vegetable Stir-Fry

6	Protein Pancakes with Berries	Chicken and Quinoa Burrito Bowl	Grilled Shrimp and Asparagus
7	Avocado Toast with Poached Eggs	Salmon and Avocado Wrap	Black Bean and Vegetable Quesadilla
8	Quinoa Breakfast Bowl	Baked Chicken Thighs with Broccoli	Quinoa and Vegetable Stuffed Peppers
9	Protein Smoothie with Spinach	Lentil Soup with Whole Grain Bread	Turkey Meatball and Zucchini Noodles
10	Greek Yogurt with Nuts and Honey	Chickpea Salad with Feta	Grilled Tofu and Vegetable Skewers
11	Scrambled Eggs with Tomatoes	Shrimp and Quinoa Stir-Fry	Baked Cod with Lemon and Herbs
12	Protein Waffles with Greek Yogurt	Black Bean and Corn Salad	Grilled Turkey Burgers with

			Sweet Potato Fries
13	Chia Seed Pudding with Berries	Tuna Salad Lettuce Wraps	Quinoa and Kale Stuffed Bell Peppers
14	Cottage Cheese and Fruit Salad	Farro Salad with Roasted Vegetables	Lentil and Spinach Stuffed Mushrooms
15	Protein Smoothie Bowl	Grilled Chicken Caesar Salad	Baked Salmon with Dill and Garlic
16	Peanut Butter Banana Toast	Egg Salad Lettuce Wraps	Chickpea and Quinoa Buddha Bowl
17	Omelette with Veggies and Feta	Turkey and Vegetable Stir-Fry	Tofu and Broccoli Rice Bowl
18	Breakfast Burrito with Eggs	Quinoa and Chickpea Patties	Grilled Steak with Roasted Vegetables
19	Yogurt and Berry Parfait	Shrimp and Asparagus Risotto	Lentil and Vegetable Curry

20	Protein Pancakes with Syrup	Greek Salad with Grilled Chicken	Baked Cod with Mediterranean Quinoa
21	Avocado and Egg Breakfast Wrap	Quinoa and Black Bean Enchiladas	Turkey and Vegetable Skewers

Printed in Dunstable, United Kingdom